You Know You're a
Gardening Fanatic
When...

Ben Fraser

summersdale

YOU KNOW YOU'RE A GARDENING FANATIC WHEN...

Summersdale Publishers Ltd
46 West Street
Chichester
West Sussex
PO19 1RP
UK

www.summersdale.com

Printed and bound in China

ISBN: 978-1-84953-070-5

Substantial discounts on bulk quantities of Summersdale books are available to corporations, professional associations and other organisations. For details contact Summersdale Publishers by telephone: +44 (0) 1243 771107, fax: +44 (0) 1243 786300 or email: nicky@summersdale.com.

To..

From..

You spend more time in the shed than you do in the house.

Your partner buys you a leaf blower for your birthday and you think it's romantic.

You have the number of every regional garden centre on speed-dial in your mobile phone.

You name your children Freesia, Lily and Tulip – and two of them are boys.

You are investigated because of the
high number of 'pot plants' in
your home.

Upon seeing a weed, you compulsively stop to pull it up – regardless of whether it's in your garden or not.

You favour your ride-on
lawnmower over your Ferrari.

You own more pairs of gardening gloves than you do pairs of socks.

You have pin-ups of Alan Titchmarsh or Charlie Dimmock in your greenhouse – not to mention one of Monty Don in the locket around your neck.

You think multiculturalism
means mixing flowers
with vegetables.

You've installed a ringer for the telephone in your garden so you won't miss that crucial call from the seed company.

Even your Sunday best has a lingering smell of manure.

Your idea of an 'energy-saving bulb' is
a self-planting crocus.

You can talk about your 'dibber' without sniggering.

21

You take Santa at his word
and spend Christmas Day
'hoeing'.

Your leylandii hedge is so huge that, from space, it has been mistaken for the Great Wall of China.

You consider soil under one's fingernails to be a sign of good character.

You hold a full moon party so people can admire your garden at night.

You pop out for milk and return two hours later with a can of Miracle Grow and some new shears.

You're very popular with birds
– of the feathered variety.

You look like you've been wrestling
with lions after an afternoon in
the rockery.

You think God created rainy days just to give you a chance to get the housework done.

You're more proud of your spectacular
bed of roses than you are of
your children.

You think your partner is being affectionate, but they're actually just picking leaves out of your hair.

Life without *Gardeners' World*
would be totally unbearable.

You have been known to get down on your hands and knees to cut the grass with a pair of scissors and a ruler.

You spend more money on plants than you do on food for your family.

You are a firm believer that
wellies go with everything.

You refer to your plants as 'he' or 'she' and have been caught having lengthy discussions with them on numerous occasions.

You flaunt grass stains
with pride.

You spend so long immersed in your garden that your family report you as a missing person.

You think deadheading is better than a night out.

You sing your plants a night-time lullaby; 'Raindrops Keep Falling on My Head' is their favourite.

You get stopped going through airport security after they discover a trowel concealed in your hand luggage.

You rush home from work at
lunchtime to check on
the seedlings.

You have window boxes on
your car.

You have a specially allocated
gardening wardrobe, which includes
padded, soil-repellent dungarees and a
matching pair of luxury
pruning gauntlets.

You hold an annual funeral
service in your garden after
the first frost.

You spend so much money at your local garden centre they shut down whenever you're out of town.

You have a recurring nightmare about giant, black slugs.

You know more about the ingredients in your fertiliser than you do about the ingredients in your dinner.

You own a miner's hat with a light so you can garden in the dark.

You keep a spare pair of pruning shears in the boot of your car, just in case you spot a shrub along the roadside that needs a bit of TLC.

You make sweaters for your trees so they don't catch a cold in winter.

You know the difference
between soil and dirt.

You spot a rabbit eyeing-up your vegetable patch and it doesn't make you feel 'all warm and fuzzy inside'.

You sit still with a fixed grin for such long periods in the garden that your spouse thinks you've turned into a gnome.

You think talking dirty means whispering the word 'compost'.

You buy half-dead plants, because you KNOW you can save them.

You rifle through your neighbours' rubbish in the middle of the night to salvage anything you can use for compost.

66

You erect a 'Ball Games Prohibited' sign on your lawn every time the grandchildren come to visit.

You're invited to a dinner party and take along a bucket of fresh manure as a gift.

You hire a garden-sitter to keep an eye
on your 'babies' while you're away
on holiday.

You get up in the middle of the night to go snail-hunting.

You have a sign on your car that reads 'Seedlings On Board'.

You make excuses to get out of family functions to spend the day dredging the pond – it's more fun.

The staff at your local garden
centre regularly ring you
for advice.

You clean your favourite
garden tools in the
dishwasher.

You judge a person by the size of their courgettes.

You can't be trusted to go anywhere
without coming home with cuttings
stashed in your pockets.

The first thing you do in the morning
is run outside to see who
sprouted today.

For you, the gardening season begins on 1 January and ends on 31 December.

You wage war against next door's cat after discovering the unsightly deposits it has left all over your perfectly pruned lawn.

Your idea of home shopping is flicking
through your collection of
seed catalogues.

Your idea of a hot date
is mowing the lawn on a
summer's day.

You ask your family to bury you in the compost pile in the event of your death, which will probably be the result of a tragic gardening-related accident.

You insist on looking the other way
during cross-pollination to give your
plants some privacy.

You rise at 5.00 a.m. to get in some
quality gardening time before
the neighbours.

You start giving your family and friends tickets to the unveiling of the topiary as birthday gifts and wonder why they aren't more appreciative.

You step outside on the first day of spring and your spouse says, 'See you in autumn, dear.'

Your neighbours are concerned
about your trug habit.

Your family puts up a sign on the garden gate that says 'BEWARE OF THE GARDENER'.

Have you enjoyed this book?
If so, why not write a review
on your favourite website?

Thanks very much for buying
this Summersdale book.

www.summersdale.com